The Secret Language

Of The Heart

CATHERINE SERESS

ISBN - 13: 978-0-9797429-0-3
ISBN - 10: 0-9797429-0-0
Printed in China

Cover Design by Jason & Eve Alexander
Illustrations by Stephen G. Seress-Smith

To contact the author write:
Catherine Seress
P.O. Box 15368
Sarasota, Florida 34277-1368

or visit:
www.catherineseress.com
www.myspace.com/bharatiishaya
www.halopublishing.com

Halo
Publishing International®

www.halopublishing.com
6415 Granger Road, Independence, Ohio 44131

My heart dedicates this book to your heart.

My heart is born

At some point, prior to my arrival
physically separate from my mother
into this world, my heart is born.
It is of flesh and beats rhythmically,
a very mechanical function to fulfill.
It beats right now, to this day,
having not stopped once to take
breath.

My heart murmurs

They say I have a murmur,
a slight imperfection in one of the
valves which causes it to sound
like a wave, a gentle whoosh, in
between each beat. Some people
are born with holes in their heart,
so I hear. I do not know what their
hearts sound like.

I am beautiful

My heart is a blank page

My heart has no experience of you, yet. It is blank. But it becomes what you write upon it. If you write upon my heart that I am stupid, I shall be stupid. If you write upon my heart that I am beautiful, I shall be beautiful. Please be careful what you write upon my heart.

My heart whispers

My heart sees something of interest and so it calls. Because it is unsure, it whispers. It is not sure if that which it sees is good, or bad, or indifferent. So quietly it calls for that which it longs to come closer.

My heart grows big

As my body grows, so does my heart. As my life extends, so does my heart. Or so I like to think. It grows big when it fills with joy. Joy may be at the sight of a sunset or the smell of rain or a call from a friend. Sometimes it grows so big I am not sure I could fit it through a door. I can see the whole universe when my heart is big. Can you?

My heart grows small

If my heart can grow big, it must
also sometimes grow small.
It does this when it is frightened
or becomes hard from too much
breakage. My eyes squint when
my heart grows small, so I can only
see a small part of the world, of the
room, of the person. I can miss
a lot when my heart grows small.

My heart breaks

The Buddhists say this is why we
have hearts – for them to break.
I forget sometimes that it is me who
has my heart. Sometimes I think
I give it to other people and that
they break it. This is not true.
My heart is in my hands when it
breaks. Always.

My heart witnesses

My heart is not blind. Even when I close my eyes, my heart can still see. It sees all the joy, the pain, the beauty and the ugliness that there is to be seen. The names I give to what my heart witnesses will either make my heart grow larger or smaller.

My heart is quiet

When my mind is still, so is my heart. It is at peace when there is no noise from my head telling it what to do. My head will say this and that about this and that person, and this can upset my heart. Or it can open it wider. It depends on what my mind says about this or that person. It depends upon what I write on their blank page.

My heart soars

There are times when my heart soars. It rises above the clouds, into the heavens, beyond what we know of the sky and the universe. It does this when it becomes one with all. It is rare for this to happen for me. But it feels more than good... and so I tell it to soar as much as possible.

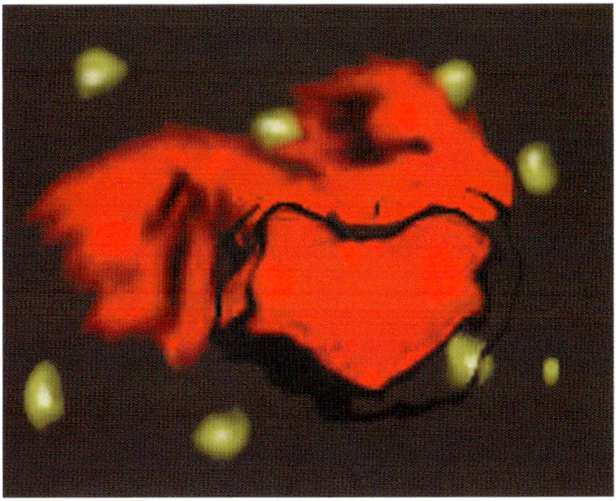

My heart is tied

When I tell my heart what to do, it cannot soar. I tether it with my desires -- with what I want -- to this world. It becomes un-free, for that is what happens if something is tied down. It is not free. Even wishing for my heart to be free does not make it so.

My heart sings

The wind is up, and clouds dance across the sky. Hoar frost covers the world that my eye sees.
My heart sings at the beauty and grandeur of the world and the magic of nature. It is singing in my chest, a light, bright melody. I do not know the words. This does not matter. It is singing. This is all that matters.

My heart crumples

An expectation, hidden even from my heart, is not met. It feels like a dent in the side of my heart when what I want does not happen. I am disappointed; my heart crumples. I can cry over the disappointment or I can remember that I was only imagining something else. Either way, my heart will pump itself into fullness at some time. I do not need to worry.

My heart bleeds

The pain of what my heart witnesses is so bad that it bleeds. It is leaking its life force and I cannot stop it. Sometimes my heart must bleed dry before it can heal. I do not enjoy my heart bleeding, but sometimes it is necessary. Only when it bleeds fully do any clots or any bad blood finally leave.

My heart aches

I am missing you. I miss seeing you, I miss hearing the sound of your voice, your laughter. I miss being able to have you close to hand. My heart aches. It is longing. It is longing for that which it cannot see. And in its longing, it aches as it stretches out towards that which does not appear to be near.

My heart trembles

I am nervous. I am unsure. My heart is dancing a dance in my chest that knows no rhythm. If my heart had rhythm, I would certainly feel sure. But I am unsure how to proceed. I am frightened of some thing. I do not know always what this thing is, but my heart imagines that it does and so it trembles.

My heart cries

My heart is lonely and so like a young child or a puppy, it cries. It is crying to be held, to be comforted. I forget sometimes that I am the comforter and what my mind thinks is what my heart feels, too. I can turn a light on in my heart and it will stop crying. I think I will do this. Now. I do not need to leave it to cry all alone in the darkness of its night.

My heart is heavy

I feel deeply sad. My heart carries a burden and so it feels very heavy. This burden may be something that does not belong to my heart. It may not be its to carry. I will look into my heart and see what burden is there. I will need to let it go. I may need to ask for help. Sometimes I am not strong enough to unburden my self alone.

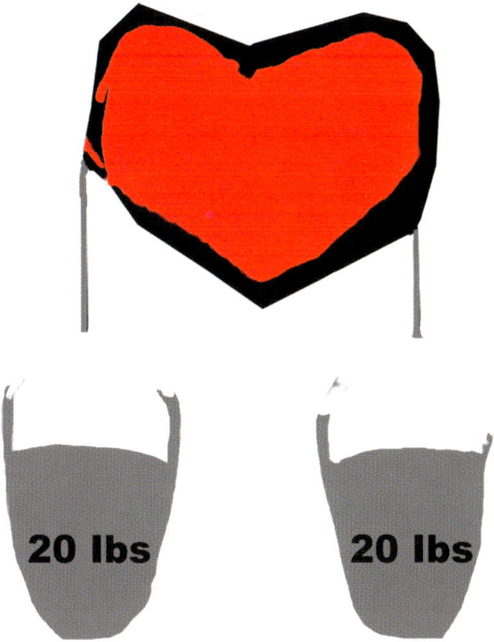
20 lbs
20 lbs

My heart is weary

For too long my heart has been a warrior without rest. It has fought the world and all that is in it.
It needs to rest for it is weary and the days have been long.
The armour it is carrying is very heavy and may not be necessary, but only when I stop fighting will my heart be able to rest. Then I may remove the armour too for a while. There may be scars or even bleeding under this armour.
It will heal if I let it rest in the warm sunshine.

My heart explodes

The ecstasy of life, of seeing your heart, makes my heart explode. Like fireworks, it shoots out dancing bright stars into the air around me. It explodes in ecstasy and supreme joy, delirious with delight. If you are awake, you will know that my heart has exploded. I hope you are awake so I can share this with you.

My heart is tight

I have a grievance, a resentment, and so my heart is tight. That which was once fleshy and moist and alive, has become desiccated ... dry ... hard ... small. My heart does not want to know that it has been mistaken. It is directed by my mind, and my mind tells it that you do not love me. That you want to hurt me or mislead me. That you do not like me. And so it becomes tight.

My heart is clear

My heart is at peace for I listen to
it. It says, "Do this," and I do this.
Often, my heart says to me,
"Do this," and I do that instead.
My mind does not always like what
my heart says to do, even if it says it
with love. I am scared sometimes
to do as my heart says. I worry that
I will do it wrong or badly.
But sometimes I listen. I am still.
My heart is clear.

My heart withdraws

What I had thought may not be true. My heart pulls back into my chest. It needs to consider, to call upon its wisdom. Or it may just be hiding. Right there, behind my bones. It does not want to come out to play with your heart. It does not want to speak to your heart. I may have been wrong. It is thinking. And thinking is not good for my heart.

My heart is black and white

I am decided. There is no excuse, no rationalisation, no logical explanation that will persuade me otherwise at this time. I know what I believe and that, my friend, is that. I know that my heart speaks the truth to me. My heart is black and white.

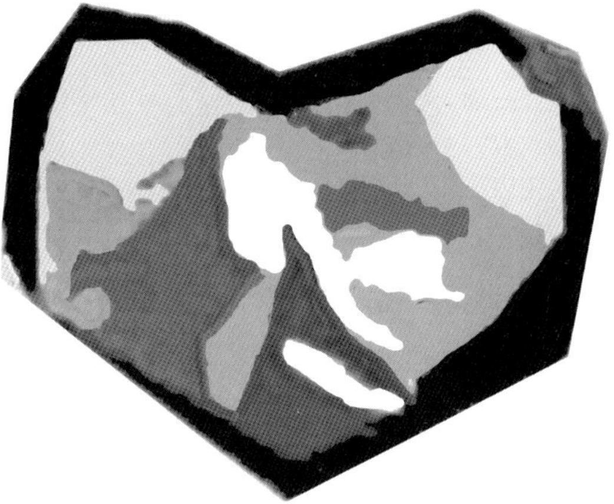

My heart is on fire

My heart is burning; I am enraged. I am too angry for words. No words like water will cool me down when my heart is on fire. I must leave the room. I will go for a walk. I will listen when the wind whispers to me, when the sun shines its rays and says to me, "Welcome, fiery heart." And maybe then I can laugh. But not now.

My heart tinkles

My heart feels a sweet, tender joy. I am quietly delighted; my mind dances with newness and possibility, hopes and dreams. It is like this when I see baby people or animals. It is like this when something good happens for my friend. Still, it is a secret kind of joy. It is my delight.

My heart quivers

You call me by my name. I look at you, my heart longing, and you respond. You touch me. I am touched. Deeply. Maybe you put my arm through yours on a walk or your eyes go past my fear into my soul. My heart is delighted and unsure, all at the same time. This can be good for my heart.

My heart shudders

You approach me with kindness,
gentleness and purpose. I know
you see my heart, past the lies my
mind and mouth would tell you.
My heart shudders in its tenderness,
somewhere between a quiver and
an earthquake. It gets the attention
of my mind. I must not think,
for thinking will put walls between
you and I.

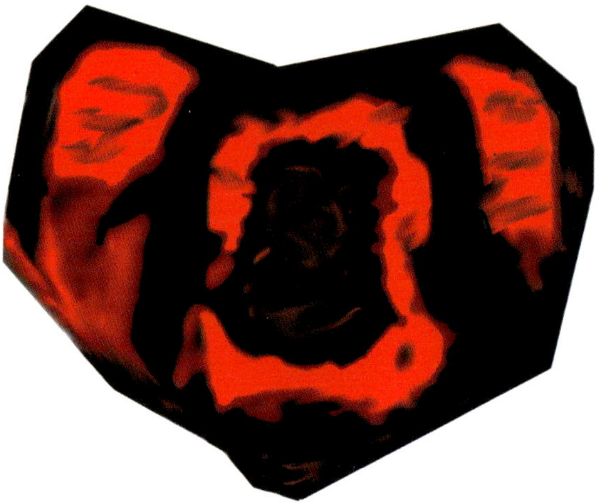

My heart barks

I do not hear my heart. So it commands me to sit up! Pay attention! Do as you are told! It orders me about so that I may hear it. And maybe, too, listen to it. The message of my heart is important. It knows this. Sometimes I forget.

My heart plays

In delight, I notice the birds
pecking at the ground. I see them,
not as hungry creatures trying to
eat so they do not die, but as
expressions of infinite beauty.
I see their feathers blowing in the
wind. I imagine their conversation.
My heart plays with the image.
It is happy.

My heart wears sneakers

I am scared. I have misused my heart's love in the past and now I am unsure. My heart is searching for its running shoes. Happily, it cannot find them. But it would like to. It would like to run away. It knows I am not yet skilled enough to handle it carefully and with love. It is frightened . . . of me.

My heart is wild

My heart is beyond rage. It has become uncontrollable. I can do nothing for now. I will have to wait. The truth will become clear. But for now, it is savage. Wild. Raw.
I must not let my heart see anyone when it is like this. I do not want to see it when it is like this. Yet it is like this. What pain is under that rage in my heart?

My heart twists

My heart is listening to my mind. My mind says this and that, and though my heart thinks that it is not true what my mind is saying, it is not sure. It is building a wall of resentment, anger, maybe even of self-pity. It wants more bricks and so it seeks other twisted hearts who will feed it the bricks of separation. This is not really my heart. It only feels this way because it has become twisted.

My heart zings

I feel excited about what is happening or about to happen. My heart zips back and forth, like a happy dog. It yaps and pants and dances on four legs. My heart wants the whole world to feel as free and happy as it does right now. I laugh with my heart. Life feels fun.

My heart grows thorns

My heart is irritated. My heart wants to be left alone, and yet it is not alone. It grows thorns to keep out the intruders, the intrusions. If untended, these thorns will overtake my heart, spiking it, piercing it. What began as protection becomes the death of my heart. I must pay attention and pull out the roots of these thorns.

My heart flowers

From the earth of humility, a small something pushes upwards.
It is relentless in its quest for life, for love, for beauty. It pushes its greenness towards the sun, towards hope. It will not hide itself nor will it be dissuaded. The bud of its rebirth appears, and the petals stretch themselves out. It is ready.

My heart bows

My heart witnesses your courage and grace. Your heart is breaking; it is all over your face. And your body. And your heart is cracking inside. Yet, you do not choose selfishly. You choose self-lessly. You give. Even though your own heart is breaking. I see this. My heart sees this. We honor you and your heart.